States
WYOMING

by Bridget Parker

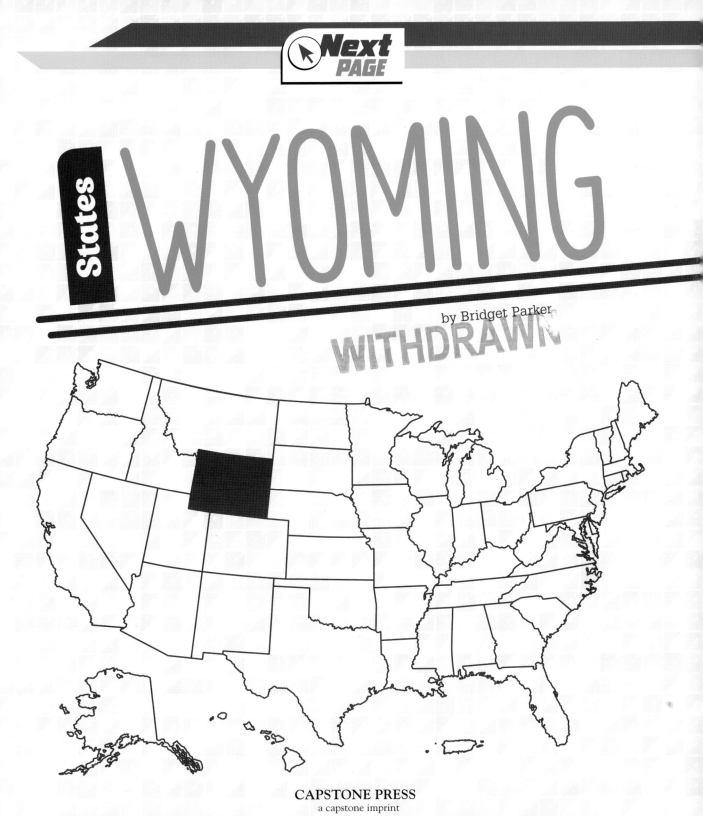

CAPSTONE PRESS
a capstone imprint

Next Page Books are published by Capstone Press,
1710 Roe Crest Drive, North Mankato, Minnesota 56003
www.mycapstone.com

Library of Congress Cataloging-in-Publication Data
Cataloging-in-publication information is on file with the Library of
Congress.
ISBN 978-1-5157-0439-3 (library binding)
ISBN 978-1-5157-0498-0 (paperback)
ISBN 978-1-5157-0550-5 (ebook PDF)

Editorial Credits
Jaclyn Jaycox, editor; Richard Korab and Katy LaVigne, designers;
Morgan Walters, media researcher; Tori Abraham, production specialist

Printed and bound in China.
0316/CA21600187
012016 009436F16

TABLE OF CONTENTS

Want to take your research further? Ask your librarian if your school subscribes to PebbleGo Next. If so, when you see this helpful symbol 🔍 throughout the book, log onto www.pebblegonext.com for bonus downloads and information.

LOCATION

Wyoming is located in the northwestern United States. Six states border Wyoming. Montana borders it on the north and northwest. South Dakota and Nebraska border Wyoming on the east. Colorado borders Wyoming to the south, and Utah lies to the southwest. Idaho makes up most of Wyoming's western border. Wyoming's capital, Cheyenne, is the state's largest city. Casper and Laramie are the next largest cities.

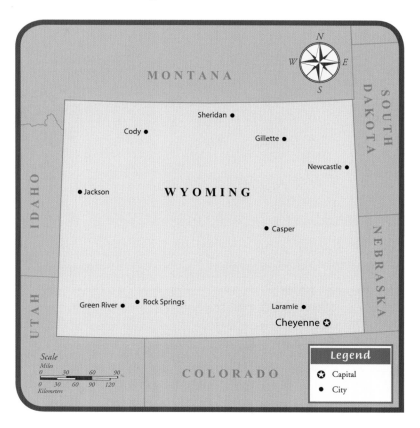

PebbleGo Next Bonus! To print and label your own map, go to www.pebblegonext.com and search keywords: **WY MAP**

Wyoming is the least populated state in the country.

GEOGRAPHY

Mountain ranges fill much of Wyoming. The Rocky Mountains lie in western Wyoming. Gannett Peak in the Wind River Range is the state's highest point. It is 13,804 feet (4,207 meters) above sea level. The state's largest lakes are in the mountain regions. Yellowstone Lake is located in Yellowstone National Park.

Basins are low, flat lands between Wyoming's mountain ranges. These spots are also called holes. The Great Divide Basin is dry and windy. In places, the wind even carries in sand and forms dunes.

The Great Plains sit south of the Bighorn Mountains and the Black Hills. Grassy, open land covers this eastern part of the state.

PebbleGo Next Bonus! To watch a video about Yellowstone National Park, go to www.pebblegonext.com and search keywords:

WY VIDEO

Grand Teton National Park is home to lakes, valleys, rivers, and the highest peaks of the Teton Mountain range.

Yellowstone National Park is the oldest national park in the United States.

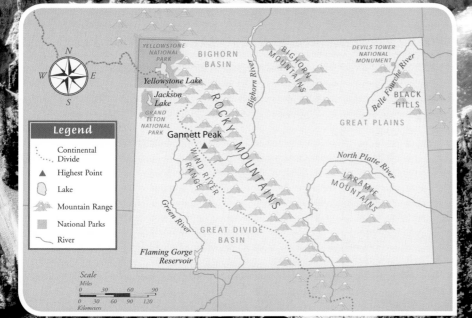

Legend

- ┈┈ Continental Divide
- ▲ Highest Point
- Lake
- Mountain Range
- National Parks
- River

YELLOWSTONE NATIONAL PARK

BIGHORN BASIN

BIGHORN MOUNTAINS

DEVILS TOWER NATIONAL MONUMENT

Belle Fourche River

BLACK HILLS

Yellowstone Lake

Jackson Lake

Bighorn River

GRAND TETON NATIONAL PARK

Gannett Peak

ROCKY MOUNTAINS

GREAT PLAINS

WIND RIVER RANGE

North Platte River

LARAMIE MOUNTAINS

Green River

GREAT DIVIDE BASIN

Flaming Gorge Reservoir

Scale
Miles
0   30   60   90
0 30 60 90 120
Kilometers

WEATHER

Wyoming's temperatures vary with land elevation. In mountain areas, the July temperature averages 59 degrees Fahrenheit (15 degrees Celsius). On the plains, the average July temperature is 71°F (22°C). Winter temperatures average 21°F (-6°C).

Average High and Low Temperatures (Cheyenne, WY)

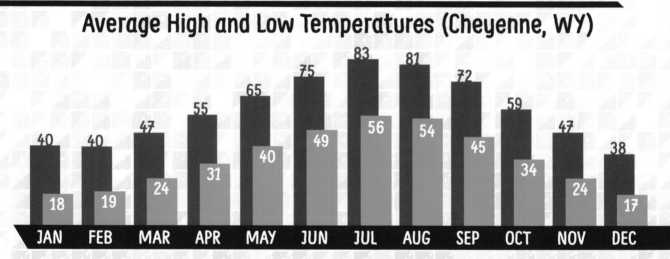

JAN	FEB	MAR	APR	MAY	JUN	JUL	AUG	SEP	OCT	NOV	DEC
40	40	47	55	65	75	83	81	72	59	47	38
18	19	24	31	40	49	56	54	45	34	24	17

LANDMARKS

Yellowstone National Park

Possibly the first national park in the world, Yellowstone is known for "Old Faithful" and other geysers as well as its wildlife herds.

Jackson Hole

This low valley sits beside the Teton range of the Rocky Mountains. It is known for its beautiful scenery and outdoor activities. Many dude ranches are found near Jackson Hole.

Devils Tower

This rock structure in the Black Hills stands 1,267 feet (386 m) taller than the land around it. The vertical grooves of the tower have many legends associated with it. One tale says a giant bear's claws scratched the rock.

HISTORY AND GOVERNMENT

John Colter was the first man to see the hot springs and geysers of Yellowstone.

American Indians lived in Wyoming thousands of years ago. By 1800 several groups lived there, including the Shoshone, Sioux, and Arapaho tribes. In 1803 France sold land including Wyoming to the United States. This sale was called the Louisiana Purchase.

John Colter explored Yellowstone in 1807. Westbound travelers passed through Wyoming in the mid-1800s. The railroad reached Wyoming in the late 1860s.

Wyoming Territory was created in 1868. In 1869 the territory gave women the right to vote and hold office. Women did not have these rights anywhere else in the country. Wyoming became the 44th U.S. state in 1890.

Today Wyoming's government has executive, legislative, and judicial branches. The governor leads the executive branch. Wyoming's Senate has 30 members. The House of Representatives has 60 members. The Senate and House form the legislative branch. Judges make up the judicial branch along with the courts system.

Wyoming's state capitol building became an official National Historic Landmark in 1987.

INDUSTRY

Tourism to the state's mountains and national parks is an important service industry for Wyoming. But Wyoming is mostly a cattle state. Beef cattle and calves are the top livestock products. Farming of sugar beets, hay, and other crops also contributes to the state economy.

Wyoming is not a big manufacturing state. Some mining and agricultural products are processed in the state. Soda ash, petroleum products, and refined beet sugar are examples of this.

About 70 percent of Wyoming's agricultural income comes from livestock and livestock products.

Mining is a top industry for the state. Wyoming is a leading state for coal production and uranium. It also has petroleum, natural gas, bentonite, trona, and platinum.

Eight of the 10 largest coal mines in the United States are found in Wyoming.

POPULATION

Wyoming is not a hugely populated state. Less than 600,000 people live there. If you spread them out, there would be about five or six people per square mile (two to three people per square kilometer). New Jersey would have more than 1,200 people per square mile (465 per square kilometer).

At least 85 percent of Wyoming's population is white. Almost 9 percent is Hispanic. More than 10,000 American Indians live in Wind River Reservation. The state also has a small population of African-Americans. Many new residents come to the state for its mining jobs and outdoor recreation.

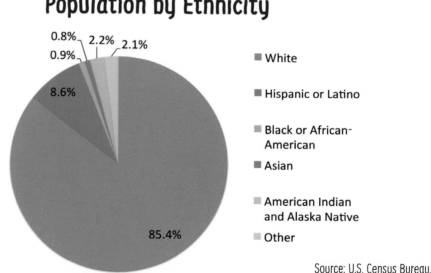

Population by Ethnicity

0.8% 2.2% 2.1%
0.9%
8.6%
85.4%

- White
- Hispanic or Latino
- Black or African-American
- Asian
- American Indian and Alaska Native
- Other

Source: U.S. Census Bureau.

FAMOUS PEOPLE

Patricia MacLachlan (1938–) is an author of children's books. She won the Newbery Medal for *Sarah, Plain and Tall* (1985). She was born in Cheyenne.

Richard Bruce "Dick" Cheney (1941–) is a former vice president of the United States. He served from 2001 to 2009. He was raised near Casper.

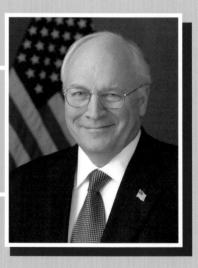

Nellie Tayloe Ross (1876–1977) was Wyoming's governor from 1925 to 1927. She was the nation's first female governor and also the first woman to lead the U.S. Mint (1933–1953).

James Cash Penney (1875–1971) started the JCPenney department stores in Kemmerer. Shopping malls all across the United States have JCPenney stores.

William F. "Buffalo Bill" Cody (1846–1917) founded the town of Cody. He was famous for his Wild West Show.

Chief Washakie (1798–1900) was a Shoshone leader. He worked to get land and social services for his people. His policy of peace toward the U.S. government helped the Shoshone gain a large reservation in central Wyoming.

STATE SYMBOLS

Tree

plains cottonwood

Flower

Indian paintbrush

Bird

meadowlark

Butterfly

Sheridan's green hairstreak

PebbleGo Next Bonus! To make a snack great for hiking in Wyoming, go to www.pebblegonext.com and search keywords:
WY RECIPE

Gemstone

jade

Reptile

horned toad

Animal

bison

Coin

Sacagawea golden dollar coin

Grass

western wheatgrass

Fossil

knightia

FAST FACTS

STATEHOOD
1890

CAPITAL ☆
Cheyenne

LARGEST CITY •
Cheyenne

SIZE
97,093 square miles (251,470 square kilometers) land area
(2010 U.S. Census Bureau)

POPULATION
582,658 (2013 U.S. Census estimate)

STATE NICKNAME
Big Wyoming, Equality State, Cowboy State

STATE MOTTO
"Equal Rights"

STATE SEAL

Images on Wyoming's state seal represent important ideas and the economy in the state. A statue of a woman holds a banner with the state's motto "Equal Rights." Four of Wyoming's major industries, livestock, mines, oil, and grain, are shown on scrolls around pillars. The two men are a rancher and a miner. The number 44 can be spotted on the shield. Wyoming was the 44th state to join the United States. The eagle above the number stands for the United States. There are two years on the seal, 1869 and 1890. In 1869 the territorial government was organized. Wyoming became a state in 1890. Wyoming's state seal was adopted in 1893.

PebbleGo Next Bonus! To print and color your own flag, go to www.pebblegonext.com and search keywords:

WY FLAG

STATE FLAG

Wyoming adopted its flag on January 31, 1917. The red border represents Wyoming's American Indians and the blood of those wounded or killed in battle. The white stripe stands for purity and goodness. The blue rectangle on the flag stands for justice. A bison is in the center of the flag. The state seal is on the bison. The seal shows a statue of a woman holding a banner with the state's motto, "Equal Rights." Four scrolls show the state's major industries. A rancher and a miner also face each other on the seal. The dates 1869 and 1890 honor when Wyoming became a territory and a state.

MINING PRODUCTS

natural gas, coal, petroleum, soda ash, bentonite, helium, sand and gravel

MANUFACTURED GOODS

petroleum and coal products, chemicals, fabricated metals, nonmetallic mineral products, food products, machinery

FARM PRODUCTS

cattle and calves, hogs, hay, sugar beets, corn

PebbleGo Next Bonus! To learn the lyrics to the state song, go to www.pebblegonext.com and search keywords:
WY SONG

WYOMING TIMELINE

1620 The Pilgrims establish a colony in the New World in present-day Massachusetts.

1800s Shoshone, Crow, Sioux, Cheyenne, and Arapaho American Indians are living in Wyoming.

1807 John Colter is the first white man known to explore Wyoming.

1812 Robert Stuart discovers South Pass as a way to cross the Rocky Mountains.

 **1834** William Sublette and Robert Campbell open the first permanent trading post in Wyoming.

 **1861–1865** The Union and the Confederacy fight the Civil War.

 **1868** Wyoming becomes a U.S. territory.

 **1868** The U.S. government creates the Wind River Reservation for the Shoshone tribe.

 **1869** Wyoming's territorial government gives Wyoming women the right to vote.

 **1890** Wyoming becomes the 44th state on July 10.

 **1914–1918** World War I is fought; the United States enters the war in 1917.

 **1925** Wyoming governor Nellie Tayloe Ross becomes the first female governor in the United States.

 **1939–1945**   World War II is fought; the United States enters the war in 1941.

 1958   Warren Air Force Base near Cheyenne becomes the nation's first intercontinental ballistic missile site.

 **1988**   Forest fires sweep through much of Yellowstone National Park.

Wyoming resident Rulon Gardner wins the 2000 Summer Olympic gold medal in Greco-Roman wrestling.

2010

Yellowstone National Park sets a record for number of visitors in a month. July 2010 has 957,000 visitors.

2015

Scientists discover that the Yellowstone supervolcano system could be more than five times larger than previously known.

Glossary

basin *(BAY-suhn)*—an area of land around a river from which water drains into the river

dune *(DOON)*—a hill or ridge of sand piled up by the wind

elevation *(el-uh-VAY-shuhn)*—the height above seal level

executive *(ig-ZE-kyuh-tiv)*—the branch of government that makes sure laws are followed

geyser *(GYE-zur)*—an underground spring that shoots hot water and steam through a hole in the ground

industry *(IN-duh-stree)*—a business which produces a product or provides a service

legislature *(LEJ-iss-lay-chur)*—a group of elected officials who have the power to make or change laws for a country or state

petroleum *(puh-TROH-lee-uhm)*—an oily liquid found below the earth's surface used to make gasoline, heating oil, and many other products

recreation *(rek-ree-AY-shuhn)*—the games, sports, hobbies, etc., that people enojy in their spare time

sea level *(SEE LEV-uhl)*—the average level of the surface of the ocean, used as a starting point from which to measure the height or depth of any place

tourism *(TOOR-i-zuhm)*—the business of taking care of visitors to a country or place

Read More

Felix, Rebecca. *What's Great About Wyoming?* Our Great States. Minneapolis: Lerner Publications, 2016.

Ganeri, Anita. *United States of America: A Benjamin Blog and His Inquisitive Dog Guide.* Country Guides. Chicago: Heinemann Raintree, 2015.

Petreycik, Rick. *Wyoming.* It's My State! New York: Cavendish Square Publishing, 2016.

Internet Sites

FactHound offers a safe, fun way to find Internet sites related to this book. All of the sites on FactHound have been researched by our staff.

Here's all you do:

Visit *www.facthound.com*

Type in this code: 9781515704393

Check out projects, games and lots more at
www.capstonekids.com

Critical Thinking Using the Common Core

1. The state sport of Wyoming is rodeo. It's a contest in which people ride horses and bulls and rope cattle. Would this be something you would like to try? Why or why not? (Integration of Knowledge and Ideas)

2. What are the two average July temperatures in Cheyenne, Wyoming? (Key Ideas and Details)

3. Wyoming's mining products include natural gas, coal, petroleum, and soda ash, among others. What is petroleum? (Craft and Structure)

Index